Dream by Design Journal

How the Power of One Year Can Build Your Dreams

By **Art Sepúlveda** *and <u>You</u>!*

Dream by Design Journal: How the Power of One Year Can Build Your Dreams
Copyright © 2009 by Art Sepúlveda
550 Queen Street
Honolulu, Hawaii 96813

International Standard Book Number: 978-0-9819312-1-0

Project Management and Media Consultants: Vaughn Street, LLC.
www.vaughnstreet.com

COVER AND INTERIOR DESIGN:
Eastco Multi Media Solutions
3646 California Road
Orchard Park, NY 14127
www.eastcomultimedia.com

Printed in Canada

Introduction

A Dream Year

Congratulations on your decision to dream by design!

Remember this simple and thought-provoking phrase:

> It takes a dream to wake up your faith, but it takes faith to make your dream come true.

Faith can begin with the simple belief that God unconditionally loves you and that you were born for a bright future. You see, to dream by design is to understand that no person's birth is an "accident" or "mistake."

I remind you of this because as you move forward, you'll encounter resistance, both internal and external. Some weeks you'll make great progress, and some weeks you may make mistakes or experience perceived setbacks. External circumstances may require patient determination or even some course correction.

Your journal is formatted in fifty-two sections, or steps, so you can dream by design, in the power of one year. I'd like to encourage you to work through one section per week, but there are really no rules for this journal. Some people may move more quickly, while others move more slowly. The main issue is to keep moving forward toward your dreams.

Don't think of your journal as another item on your to-do list! It is a place of inspiration for your daily life. Simply get in the habit of opening your journal each day. In each section, you'll find a series of quotes, scriptures, questions, and actions. Take time to meditate on the quotes and scriptures. Don't be in a hurry to answer the questions—in fact, some of them may take several days of thought and prayer to answer.

As you progress, you'll choose action items to move you closer to your dreams. Again, we are not just making task lists—every day is a step in your adventure!

If you have not already read my book *Dream by Design,* upon which this journal is based, I encourage you to get a copy. You'll find it a valuable companion resource filled with encouragement for your adventure.

Perhaps you've never written down your ideas and thoughts in a prayerful and soul-searching way. I believe you'll find the experience challenging, yet rewarding. As you fill in these pages, you're actually painting your future. Stick with it—the world needs you to dream by design.

Let's begin the journey, dreamer!

Art Sepúlveda

You crown the year with Your goodness,
and Your paths drip with abundance.
PSALM 65:11

1

> Deep within man dwells those slumbering
> powers; powers that would astonish him; that he
> never dreamed of possessing; forces that would
> revolutionize his life if aroused and put into action.[1]
> —ORISON SWETT MARDEN

What does the following statement mean to you with regard to your own dreams: *It takes a dream to wake up your faith, but it takes faith to make your dream come true.*

_____

_____

_____

_____

_____

_____

_____

_____

_____

When you think about dreams and goals, how does your faith come into play? Be honest!

_____

_____

_____

_____

_____

_____

_____

_____

You must have a dream to be fully alive.
The Bible says in Proverbs 29:18, "Where there
is no vision, the people perish" (KJV).

Take some time over the next few days and consider this question: Do you really believe that you can see your dreams become reality? Why or why not?

2

Hope deferred makes the heart sick.
—PROVERBS 13:12

Have you had dreams in the past that have been unfulfilled? List some below:

_____

_____

_____

_____

_____

_____

_____

_____

_____

_____

_____

How has this affected your faith?

_____

_____

_____

_____

_____

_____

_____

_____

_____

_____

If you have a dream that stays dormant and never comes to pass, you become weak and "sickly" because your life has no direction. Internally, you become dysfunctional, disappointed, and disillusioned.

Look for areas of your heart that have been "sick." How has this principle affected your hope? Your outlook on dreams? Your future?

_____

_____

_____

_____

_____

_____

_____

_____

_____

_____

_____

_____

_____

_____

_____

_____

_____

_____

_____

_____

_____

_____

3 |

Hope deferred makes the heart sick, but
when the desire comes, it is a tree of life.
—Proverbs 13:12

List some ways you have personally seen your hopes and desires
come to pass.

Dreams don't come by chance or die by accident.
So accept the fact that you're in for a battle and that you
may experience some setbacks along the path to fulfillment.
However, for every setback there can be a comeback.

Describe the feelings you experienced from these victories. And note the challenges you faced in seeing them happen.

4

Some people have a picture in their mind
right now that is simply a painting of their
circumstances. They've grown too accustomed to
the scenery of this old picture. To keep your dream
from dying, you must paint a new picture on
the canvas of your heart. That's what vision is.

What circumstances need changing in your current "picture"?

_____

_____

_____

_____

_____

_____

_____

_____

_____

_____

_____

_____

_____

_____

_____

_____

_____

_____

_____

_____

_____

What's the dream picture of your life? Take some time today, and the next few days, to "paint a new picture" of your life by describing it below.

5

**How do we start to embrace our dreams
from God's perspective? Faith.**

Do you believe God loves you? Why?

_____

_____

_____

_____

_____

_____

_____

_____

_____

Do you believe God cares about your dreams and your everyday life?
Why?

_____

_____

_____

_____

_____

_____

_____

_____

_____

_____

_____

**Your faith in God can turn your world around.
It is absolutely the most amazing force.**

Looking back on your life, how has your faith in God been a part (or not been a part) of fulfilling your dreams and overcoming challenges?

_____

_____

_____

_____

_____

_____

_____

_____

_____

_____

_____

_____

_____

_____

_____

_____

_____

_____

_____

_____

_____

_____

_____

6 Faith doesn't stay sad. Faith doesn't stay mad. Faith gets up and gets going again. This is called "fighting the good fight of faith" (1 Tim. 6:12).

What sadness or frustration do you have when thinking about unfulfilled dreams and desires?

_____

_____

_____

_____

_____

_____

_____

_____

_____

What sadness or frustration do you have regarding your present circumstances?

_____

_____

_____

_____

_____

_____

_____

_____

_____

_____

If you are going to be a dreamer and choose to live out your dreams, you will have to learn to fight this fight with all your heart and mind.

Write out a prayer to God regarding these areas. Use this as an opportunity to bring your heart, and your dreams, to Him.

7

It takes a dream to wake up your faith,
but it takes faith to make your dream come true.

Based on your journey so far, what does this principle mean to you now?

God gives you a dream to wake up your potential, to wake up your faith. What do I mean by that? To wake up your faith in God; to wake up your faith in yourself.

How has your faith been awakened through this journey?

_____

_____

_____

_____

_____

_____

_____

_____

_____

_____

_____

_____

_____

_____

_____

_____

_____

_____

_____

8

Delight yourself also in the LORD, and He shall give you the desires of your heart.
—PSALM 37:4

Now that your faith in God's plan for you is increasing, let's look more closely at your dreams. Based on what you've written down earlier and the clarity you are receiving, list the top ten dreams for your life.

Your dream succeeds when you understand it is God's gift to you. If you can do it with the ability that you have, it is probably not God's dream.

Review your list this week. Add, subtract, and modify your list—rewriting it below. Take some time here and invite God into the conversation.

9

What are dream shifts? A dream shift is the
transition, or clarification, of God's unique plan
for us as opposed to our self-willed ideas.

Looking back on your life, how have you seen your dreams and goals "shift" through the years? (For example, from high school to college, from selfish to service, from prideful to humble, etc.)

How we look at our desires is so important. We all have free will and can use the coming year to go after all kinds of goals, but how do you know what to pursue? A dream succeeds when you first understand that your dream is never just about you. Dreams involve you and bless you, but they will ultimately affect other people in a most positive and humbling way.

Look over your list on the previous pages with this in mind. How might this cause you to question some items on your list? How might it build your confidence in pursuing your dreams?

10

We humans keep brainstorming options and
plans, but GOD's purpose prevails.
—PROVERBS 19:21, THE MESSAGE

Ideas come and go. But when you choose to believe
that real dreams come from someone wiser and
greater than you, someone who wants only the
best for your life, you begin to live by faith. And
sometimes you'll see or fill your dreams begin to shift.

Take some time with your list and ask God to help you discern, or
refine, the dreams that are from Him for this season of your life.
Write your impressions below.

_____

_____

_____

_____

_____

_____

_____

_____

_____

_____

_____

_____

_____

_____

_____

_____

_____

_____

_____

Most people wonder if they ever hear God's
voice—but if you're experiencing a dream
shift, you are hearing from God!

Rewrite your refined list below.

_____

_____

_____

_____

_____

_____

_____

_____

_____

_____

_____

_____

_____

_____

_____

_____

_____

_____

_____

_____

_____

_____

_____

11

Your dream is unfolding every day. What you do today is setting you up for success tomorrow. The good news is this; God wants you to enjoy the journey. You are on your way, and God wants you to succeed more than you do!

How are you feeling about what you've been writing? Excited? Humbled? Convicted? Confident? Write about it below.

_____

_____

_____

_____

_____

_____

_____

_____

_____

_____

_____

_____

_____

_____

_____

_____

_____

_____

_____

People often pray prayers that show their wrong
thinking about this: "Lord, help me to fulfill my dream."
They are praying as if God is their opponent, trying
to hold them back from their dream. But He is not
their obstacle, and He is not your obstacle.

Are you ready to approach your dreams with confidence and faith?
Why or why not?

_____

_____

_____

_____

_____

_____

_____

_____

_____

_____

_____

_____

_____

_____

_____

_____

_____

_____

_____

_____

12

A dream comes [to pass by] much activity [work].
—ECCLESIASTES 5:3

Your dreams are coming into clearer focus, and your faith is strengthening. The foundation is ready to be built upon. Are you ready to work on your dreams? Is your energy level high? Why or why not?

_____

_____

_____

_____

_____

_____

_____

_____

_____

_____

Take a few days and examine your daily life and your calendar. Are you burning the candle at both ends? Do you have the time, energy, and resources to go after something new?

_____

_____

_____

_____

_____

_____

_____

_____

_____

Remember, you did not receive your dream because
of your natural abilities and talent. We must look to God
as our source of strength to complete the journey.

What changes must you make in your daily life in order to "make room" for dreaming by design? How can you build up your energy and faith on a weekly basis?

_____

_____

_____

_____

_____

_____

_____

_____

_____

_____

_____

_____

_____

_____

_____

_____

_____

_____

_____

_____

_____

_____

13

Some people are involved in areas that don't seem connected to God: science, technology, politics, finance, athleticism. What does God know about that? Well, He created the universe. He created you.

It's so easy to launch out toward our goals in our own effort—without making God our "senior partner." So far along this journey, how connected with God have your efforts been?

A dream succeeds when you rely on God's power to build it.
Your dream is a gift, and along with that gift, God will
also provide everything you need to see it come to pass.
The power is there if you seek it.

How can your relationship with God become more connected to your
dreaming by design?

_____

_____

_____

_____

_____

_____

_____

_____

_____

_____

_____

_____

_____

_____

_____

_____

_____

_____

_____

_____

_____

14

The tragedy of life is not so much what men suffer,
but rather what they miss.[2]
—THOMAS CARLYLE

We've spent a good amount of time building a foundation of faith and allowing God to work "dream shifts." Now, think about what *limitations* you might be putting on your dreams. Look over your list and imagine each dream expanded to levels you haven't considered before. Have you been limiting yourself? Write your impressions below.

_____

_____

_____

_____

_____

_____

_____

_____

_____

What might be the cause of these self-imposed limitations? (Poor self-esteem, failure, past hurts, rejection, bad habits, abusive words or actions, etc.)

_____

_____

_____

_____

_____

_____

_____

_____

Pushing beyond average is a choice each of us must make individually. Those who do not expect anything are never disappointed. The great news, which most people don't know, is that God has always encouraged His people to raise their level of expectation for life.

How can you, with God's help, address these limiting issues in your life?

_____

_____

_____

_____

_____

_____

_____

_____

_____

_____

_____

_____

_____

_____

_____

_____

_____

_____

_____

_____

15

Encouragement, hope, joy, creativity, positive motivation, promise, inspiration, and vision are doorways to bust you out of the box.

Are these "doorways" a part of your life? How can you access these in your life this week?

Raise your expectancy and guard it. The atmosphere of expectancy is the breeding ground for miracles!

You've written and rewritten your dreams several times already, and it's for good reason! Now, based on what you've gleaned from this section, rewrite your top dreams with appropriate expansion from those old limitations.

16 |

"For I know the plans I have for you," declares the LORD, "plans to prosper you and not to harm you, plans to give you hope and a future."
—JEREMIAH 29:11, NIV

By now, your confidence in your dreams and in the Dream Giver has grown. From your latest list of dreams, pick three that you can make significant progress on this year. This is probably not a time to write "retire in Fiji" or "visit the International Space Station." For this year, choose important "starter" dreams, or break down "bigger" dreams into "smaller" ones.

Take some time for prayer and reflection on this for the next few days.

1. _____
   _____
   _____
   _____
   _____

2. _____
   _____
   _____
   _____
   _____

3. _____
   _____
   _____
   _____
   _____

With God all things are possible.
—MARK 10:27

You've just written down three dreams. This is a big step in seeing your dreams realized. How does it feel? Scary? Exciting? Both? Can you sense the power you have tapped in to by increasing your faith in God and in your dreams?

Dreaming by Design

Your dreams, your faith, and your life are coming into focus.

To help you see the path ahead, here's an example of a pretty big dream. It has several elements that make it more than just a "wish." And it's going to take some time and effort.

Example Dream

This year I want to take our youth group on a trip to the Gulf Coast. It's the perfect setting to talk about life lessons and encourage the kids to make good choices. (Helping kids thrive and gain confidence is so amazing.) Besides, I love this area and haven't been there since I was a kid!

Your dreams may be nothing like this. Just keep in mind what we've learned about the characteristics of real dreams.

Going back to the example dream above, this is a sizable endeavor. It's big enough to be compelling and big enough to never get done. That's why we're going "see" it in the power of one year and break it down into manageable pieces. Remember, your dreams will be tested and maybe even adjusted, but your persistence is crucial.

I've listed twelve steps for this example, representing twelve months.

Example Dream

1. Write down how this dream looks—2–3 pages on all the "Who, What, Where, and Why."

2. Talk to other leaders—be open to new ideas, and don't be discouraged!

3. Pick locations and lodging—contact other churches.

4. Estimate budgets.

5. Brainstorm fund-raising ideas.

6. Talk to parents and youth at next meeting.

7. Recruit other leaders with similar appreciation for humanitarian help and interests in helping kids.

8. Visit sites myself—fun! Write down the "agenda items" I want to share with kids. How can this be an amazing, memorable time?

9. Meet with other leaders—discuss and delegate.

10. Buy supplies.

11. Next meeting—do a test-run of setup (tools, teams, training).

12. Experience a week on the Gulf Coast with our youth, serving others!

You can see both work and faith in play above. But if your motives are right, you can keep pressing as your dreams unfold. Keep your eyes open for faith challenges, and "dream shifts," along the way.

17

So then faith comes by hearing, and
hearing by the word of God.
—ROMANS 10:17

For each of your dream goals, write at least one Scripture verse that
you believe applies to that dream. (Write out the complete verse.)

1. _____
_____
_____
_____
_____
_____

2. _____
_____
_____
_____
_____
_____

3. _____
_____
_____
_____
_____
_____

Faith doesn't just happen. It grows in you.
And when it begins to develop on the inside,
it then starts to affect things around you.

Say each verse aloud now and daily—throughout the week. Don't simply read them silently—speak them with boldness.

How have these scriptures affected your faith?

_____

_____

_____

_____

_____

_____

_____

_____

_____

_____

_____

_____

_____

_____

_____

_____

_____

_____

_____

_____

18

There will be steps on this journey that you can achieve as you take action each day. But the foundation of your actions is faith. There will be steps on this journey that are bigger than you can make happen with your own abilities. But the foundation of your dream is faith.

Based on how your dreams are being clarified and refined, write down dream number one in its latest descriptive form. (That's why you keep writing down your dreams!)

_____

_____

_____

_____

Now we're going to look at the coming year and your dream design. Start by writing the outcome of your dream on line 12, and fill in the rest of the lines as you see them unfolding. You might want to start at the end and dream backward, or you might want to start with today and design forward, or a combination of both.

As you write down your dream by design in the power of one year, keep in mind there is no "right way" to do this. The key is that you believe, to the point of taking action—and writing is a powerful action!

Dream One

1. _____

_____

2. _____

_____

3. _____

_____

4. _____

_____

5. _____

_____

6. _____

_____

7. _____

_____

8. _____

_____

9. _____

_____

10. _____

_____

11. _____

_____

12. _____

_____

Congratulations! I suspect that you are feeling exhilarated by this process. Remember that these things you have written are not set in stone—dreams can come into clearer focus over time. And like any good movie, you enjoy the twists and turns, and you don't really want to know how it ends…as long as it ends well!

19

What you experience here is the power of actually believing in your dreams to the point of making them a part of your daily life. Your path may change, but your faith can stay strong. These are not "to do" lists, because your dream is more than just a goal.

Based on how your dreams are being clarified and refined, write down dream number two in its latest descriptive form. (That's why you keep writing down your dreams!)

_____

_____

_____

_____

_____

_____

_____

_____

_____

Again, start by writing the outcome of your dream on line 12, and fill in the rest of the lines as you see them unfolding. You might want to start at the end and dream backward, or you might want to start with today and design forward, or a combination of both.

Remember, the key is that you believe, to the point of taking action—and writing is a powerful action!

Dream Two

1. _____

_____

2. _____

_____

3. _____

_____

4. _____

_____

5. _____

_____

6. _____

_____

7. _____

_____

8. _____

_____

9. _____

_____

10. _____

_____

11. _____

_____

12. _____

_____

20

Faith changes things. Faith is the greatest catalyst
for change known to humanity. The struggle
we have is fitting this truth into the context
of what we think is the reality of our life.

Based on how your dreams are being clarified and refined, write down dream number three in its latest descriptive form. (That's why you keep writing down your dreams!)

_____

_____

_____

_____

_____

_____

_____

Again, start by writing the outcome of your dream on line 12, and fill in the rest of the lines as you see them unfolding. You might want to start at the end and dream backward, or you might want to start with today and design forward, or a combination of both.

Dream Three

1. _____

_____

2. _____

_____

3. _____

_____

4. _____

_____

5. _____

_____

6. _____

_____

7. _____

_____

8. _____

_____

9. _____

_____

10. _____

_____

11. _____

_____

12. _____

_____

For the eyes of the LORD run to and fro throughout
the whole earth, to show Himself strong on behalf
of those whose heart is loyal to Him.
—2 CHRONICLES 16:9

21

A faithful man will abound with blessings.
—PROVERBS 28:20

Let's begin acting on our faith by working on the first step of your dream number one. List that step here:

_____

_____

_____

_____

_____

_____

_____

_____

_____

_____

_____

_____

_____

_____

_____

_____

_____

_____

_____

_____

_____

_____

_____

_____

_____

_____

_____

_____

Take time this week to make progress toward this step. Daily effort is best, but not always possible. The point is to keep making progress—no matter how small. On the lines below, break up this step into action items, and track your progress this week.

22

If you're going to walk by faith, you cannot be afraid of skinning your knees or making a mistake or stumbling along the way.

Looking back on your efforts, what battles have you faced? What victories have you had?

_____

_____

_____

_____

_____

_____

_____

_____

_____

_____

If you've made mistakes or had slower than expected progress, how have you handled this personally?

_____

_____

_____

_____

_____

_____

_____

_____

_____

_____

What have you learned about your dream this week?

_____

_____

_____

_____

_____

_____

_____

_____

_____

What have you learned about yourself?

_____

_____

_____

_____

_____

_____

_____

_____

_____

Your dreams prove you have a design. They are given to
you from God. Why is this important? Because when
you are faced with adversity, if you believe your dream
is nothing more than a nice wish, you'll slow down,
give up, and miss out on what is possible this year.

23

Your dream is bigger than a wish. It is a gift for your life. When you believe that, you have a whole new perspective, a real belief, that your dream has its foundations in something bigger than you. And that's great news.

Let's begin acting on our faith by working on the first step of your dream number two. List that step here:

_____

_____

_____

_____

_____

_____

_____

_____

_____

_____

_____

_____

_____

_____

_____

_____

_____

_____

_____

_____

Take time this week to make progress toward this step. Daily effort is best, but not always possible. The point is to keep making progress—no matter how small. On the lines below, break up this step into action items, and track your progress this week.

24

If you're going to walk by faith, you cannot be afraid of what people might say.

Looking back on your efforts, what battles have you faced? What victories have you had?

_____

_____

_____

_____

_____

_____

_____

_____

_____

_____

If you've made mistakes or had slower than expected progress, how have you handled this personally?

_____

_____

_____

_____

_____

_____

_____

_____

_____

_____

What have you learned about your dream this week?

_____

_____

_____

_____

_____

_____

_____

_____

_____

What have you learned about yourself?

_____

_____

_____

_____

_____

_____

_____

_____

_____

Your dreams prove you have a design. They are given
to you from God. Why is this important? Because when
you are faced with adversity, if you believe your dream
is nothing more than a nice wish, you'll slow down,
give up, and miss out on what is possible this year.

25

A rocking chair moves back and forth, but it doesn't go anywhere. Author and leadership expert, John Maxwell has said, "The person who forgets the ultimate is a slave to the immediate."[3]

Let's begin acting on our faith by working on the first step of your dream number three. List that step here:

Take time this week to make progress toward this step. Daily effort is best, but not always possible. The point is to keep making progress—no matter how small. On the lines below, break up this step into action items, and track your progress this week.

26

If you're going to walk by faith, you cannot be afraid of falling short of the mark from time to time. You must press forward because your dreams are worth it.

Looking back on your efforts, what battles have you faced? What victories have you had?

_____

_____

_____

_____

_____

_____

_____

_____

_____

_____

If you've made mistakes or had slower than expected progress, how have you handled this personally?

_____

_____

_____

_____

_____

_____

_____

_____

_____

What have you learned about your dream this week?

_____

_____

_____

_____

_____

_____

_____

_____

_____

What have you learned about yourself?

_____

_____

_____

_____

_____

_____

_____

_____

_____

Your dreams prove you have a design. They are given
to you from God. Why is this important? Because
when you are faced with adversity, if you believe your
dream is nothing more than a nice wish, you'll slow down,
give up, and miss out on what is possible this year.

27

To do something different than you have ever done before so you can be someone different requires being willing to pay the price and to remove whatever obstacles are in your way.

How has your relationship to God and to other believers changed as you walk out your dreams?

Your new habit of dreaming by design begins with faith—
not faith in your willpower, effort, or intellect, but
faith in your dream and the one who gave you that dream.

Continue to work on the steps toward your dreams! In what practical ways, or different mind-sets, can you alter your approach to walking with God on this journey?

28

You can spend your life any way you want to, but you can only spend it once. God does not dictate every decision. He tells us how we should live, and then leaves the decision up to us. The decisions we make each day become the direction of our future.[4]

So far in your pursuit, have you had any "dream shifts"? Explain below.

This is a good time to stop and examine the motivations
for your dreams, because you don't want to invest your
life in something small, short-lived, and selfish.

Take time this week to prayerfully examine both your dreams and the steps you are pursuing. Should you break them down into smaller steps? What possible changes seem wise?

29

To operate in the power of one year, you must
be single-minded and settled in your design.
Then you'll be willing to make the
investments you need for your year.

With what you have learned along the way, rewrite dream number one
and any new or modified steps to fulfilling this dream.

Dream One:

Action Design:

1. _____

2. _____

3. _____

4. _____

5. _____

6. _____

7. _____

8. _____

9. _____

10. _____

11. _____

12. _____

30

Dreams don't just come to pass just because you have one. It takes effort on our part. But remember that God is for your dream coming to pass. After all, He is the author and the giver of the highest dreams that you have in your heart right now.

With what you have learned along the way, rewrite dream number two and any new or modified steps to fulfilling this dream.

Dream Two:

Action Design:

1. _____

2. _____

3. _____

4. _____

5. _____

6. _____

7. _____

8. _____

9. _____

10. _____

11. _____

12. _____

31

I call heaven and earth as witnesses today against you, that I have set before you life and death, blessing and cursing; *therefore choose life*, that both you and your descendants may live; that you may love the LORD your God, that you may obey His voice, and that you may cling to Him, for He is your life and the length of your days; and that you may dwell in the land which the LORD swore to your fathers, to Abraham, Isaac, and Jacob, to give them.
—DEUTERONOMY 30:19–20, EMPHASIS ADDED

With what you have learned along the way, rewrite dream number three and any new or modified steps to fulfilling this dream.

Dream Three:

_____

_____

_____

_____

_____

_____

_____

_____

_____

_____

_____

_____

_____

_____

_____

_____

_____

_____

Action Design:

1. _____

2. _____

3. _____

4. _____

5. _____

6. _____

7. _____

8. _____

9. _____

10. _____

11. _____

12. _____

32

Every dream needs three things. You don't own these, but you are a steward of them. What are they? The first is your time.

Your Time: Take a look at how you are utilizing your time to live your dreams. List some ways you have been investing your time wisely.

_____

_____

_____

_____

_____

_____

_____

_____

_____

_____

In what ways have you been investing poorly?

_____

_____

_____

_____

_____

_____

_____

_____

_____

You were born to imagine and do great things.
You've been given time, talent, and treasure to invest.
That inkling you feel in your heart that seems bigger
than you—that is God's investment in your life.

What changes can you make to better invest your time?

_____

_____

_____

_____

_____

_____

_____

_____

_____

_____

_____

_____

_____

_____

_____

_____

_____

_____

_____

_____

_____

33

Every dream needs three things. You don't own these, but you are a steward of them. What are they? The second is your *talent.*

Your Talent: Take a look at how you are utilizing your talents to live your dreams. List some ways you have been investing your talents.

_____

_____

_____

_____

_____

_____

_____

_____

_____

_____

In what ways have you been investing poorly?

_____

_____

_____

_____

_____

_____

_____

_____

_____

You may think your dream is small, maybe too small to really get excited about. But if you'll start to invest in your dream this year, you'll begin to see it grow.

What changes can you make to better invest your talents?

_____

_____

_____

_____

_____

_____

_____

_____

_____

_____

_____

_____

_____

_____

_____

_____

_____

_____

_____

_____

_____

_____

_____

_____

34

Every dream needs three things. You don't own these, but you are a steward of them. What are they? The third is your *treasure*.

Your Treasure: Take a look at how you are utilizing your treasures to live your dreams. List some ways you have been investing your treasure.

_____

_____

_____

_____

_____

_____

_____

_____

_____

In what ways have you been investing poorly?

_____

_____

_____

_____

_____

_____

_____

_____

_____

**Keep your eyes on your vision, and celebrate
every little step along the way!**

What changes can you make to better invest your treasure?

_____

_____

_____

_____

_____

_____

_____

_____

_____

_____

_____

_____

_____

_____

_____

_____

_____

_____

_____

_____

_____

_____

_____

_____

35

Proverbs 11:25 says, "The generous soul will be made rich, and he who waters will be watered himself." But people will curse the one who withholds.

Are you investing your time, talent, and treasure in other people's lives? As you pursue your dreams, are you helping others attain theirs? Why or why not?

Generosity is a part of being a "dream person."
Don't we all dream of being generous?

How can you start being a more generous person today? (Think about your time, talent, and treasure!)

_____

_____

_____

_____

_____

_____

_____

_____

_____

_____

_____

_____

_____

_____

_____

_____

_____

_____

_____

_____

_____

_____

_____

36

Personal achievement is nothing if it doesn't impact the lives of others.

Beyond achieving goals, what are the qualities of a "dream person" that you can move toward becoming this year?

**You want to begin this way of living right now, not
just "someday" when you've met your goals.**

As you examine how you invest your life, what motivations (both good
and bad) come to light?

_____

_____

_____

_____

_____

_____

_____

_____

_____

How might these affect your path?

_____

_____

_____

_____

_____

_____

_____

_____

_____

_____

37

There is one who scatters, yet increases more.
—Proverbs 11:24

Dreaming by design, giving, and serving all go together in the life God designed for you to live. What are three ways you can serve others as you pursue the path of your dreams?

Track your progress (and feelings in your heart) this week in the lines below.

38

As you dream by design, remember that refinement and change mean you are growing and making progress!

This week, take some time to again examine your dreams and the path you are on. With what you are learning along the way, rewrite your dream number one and the steps that you feel are best. Feel free to modify these based on what you are learning—that's the point!

Dream One:

Action Design:

1. _____

2. _____

3. _____

4. _____

5. _____

6. _____

7. _____

8. _____

9. _____

10. _____

11. _____

12. _____

Of course, continue to make daily and weekly progress on these. Every step counts! Personal notes:

_____

_____

_____

_____

39

As you dream by design, remember that refinement and change mean you are growing and making progress!

This week, take some time to again examine your dreams and the path you are on. With what you are learning along the way, rewrite your dream number two and the steps that you feel are best. Feel free to modify these based on what you are learning—that's the point!

Dream Two:

Action Design:

1. _____

2. _____

3. _____

4. _____

5. _____

6. _____

7. _____

8. _____

9. _____

10. _____

11. _____

12. _____

Of course, continue to make daily and weekly progress on these. Every step counts! Personal notes:

_____

_____

_____

_____

40

As you dream by design, remember that refinement and change mean you are growing and making progress!

This week, take some time to again examine your dreams and the path you are on. With what you are learning along the way, rewrite your dream number three and the steps that you feel are best. Feel free to modify these based on what you are learning—that's the point!

Dream Three:

Action Design:

1. _____

2. _____

3. _____

4. _____

5. _____

6. _____

7. _____

8. _____

9. _____

10. _____

11. _____

12. _____

Of course, continue to make daily and weekly progress on these. Every step counts! Personal notes:

_____

_____

_____

_____

41

Many people start running their race feeling excited and inspired. Then, "all of a sudden," they come to their first hurdle and are stunned.

Assess where you are on the path of your three dreams. As you continue to move forward this week, note the successes and hurdles you face.

We all face hurdles in our race, but
you can overcome every one.

Three main hurdles we face are self-doubt, lack of social position, and self-defeating words. How are you dealing with these three hurdles?

_____

_____

_____

_____

_____

_____

_____

_____

_____

_____

_____

_____

_____

_____

_____

_____

_____

_____

_____

_____

_____

_____

_____

42

The best thing you can do right now is to finish what you started last year and not let those good intentions grow stale. Your heart's been in the right place all along. You've got what it takes to finish it up, so go to it. Once the commitment is clear, you do what you can, not what you can't. The heart regulates the hands.
—2 Corinthians 8:10–12, The Message

What I am working on this week for dream number one (taken from your most recent action steps):

_____

_____

_____

_____

_____

What I am working on this week for dream number two:

_____

_____

_____

_____

What I am working on this week for dream number three:

_____

_____

_____

_____

This week, focus on making specific progress on your dreams. Note successes and challenges below.

43

For a dream comes through much activity,
And a fool's voice is known by his many words.
—ECCLESIASTES 5:3

By now your commitment is being tested. But don't confuse battle with defeat.

In what past areas of life have you struggled with commitment?

_____

_____

_____

_____

_____

_____

_____

_____

_____

Why?

_____

_____

_____

_____

_____

_____

_____

_____

There's a huge difference between interest and commitment
to a dream. When you're interested in doing something,
you only do it when it's convenient, but when you're
committed to do something, you accept no excuses.[5]
—KEN BLANCHARD

Are you really committed to your dreams for this season of your life?
Why?

_____

_____

_____

_____

_____

_____

_____

_____

_____

_____

_____

_____

_____

_____

_____

_____

_____

_____

_____

_____

_____

44

God can do anything, you know—far more
than you could ever imagine or guess or request
in your wildest dreams! He does it not by
pushing us around but by working within us,
his Spirit deeply and gently within us.
—EPHESIANS 3:20, THE MESSAGE

What I am working on this week for dream number one (taken from your most recent action steps):

_____

_____

_____

_____

_____

_____

What I am working on this week for dream number two:

_____

_____

_____

_____

_____

What I am working on this week for dream number three:

_____

_____

_____

_____

_____

This week, focus on making specific progress on your dreams, and note successes and challenges below.

45

If mistakes in a person's past were a hindrance to dreams being fulfilled, some very important events might never have happened.

We all make mistakes as we go. What mistakes (recent or long past) seem to continually try to mock your miracle this week?

_____

_____

_____

_____

_____

_____

_____

_____

_____

_____

How can you get those mistakes away from your dreams this week?

_____

_____

_____

_____

_____

_____

_____

_____

_____

_____

Don't let your mistakes mock your miracle!

This week, as you focus on making progress on your dreams, note successes and challenges below.

_____

_____

_____

_____

_____

_____

_____

_____

_____

_____

_____

_____

_____

_____

_____

_____

_____

_____

_____

_____

_____

_____

46

[Not in your own strength] for it is God Who is all the while effectually at work in you [energizing and creating in you the power and desire], both to *will* and to work for His good please *and* satisfaction *and* delight.
—PHILIPPIANS 2:13, AMP, EMPHASIS ADDED

What I am working on this week for dream number one (taken from your most recent action steps):

_____

_____

_____

_____

_____

What I am working on this week for dream number two:

_____

_____

_____

_____

What I am working on this week for dream number three:

_____

_____

_____

_____

This week, focus on making specific progress on your dreams; note successes and challenges below.

_____

_____

_____

_____

_____

_____

_____

_____

_____

_____

_____

_____

_____

_____

_____

_____

_____

_____

_____

_____

_____

_____

_____

_____

_____

_____

47

Fear causes the imagination to run wild with all sorts of "what ifs" long before the dream has even started to come to light. Fear distorts our vision. It's a misuse of our imagination and energy. Fear is the opposite of faith.

What fears (recent or long past) seem to continually try to stop you?

_____

_____

_____

_____

_____

_____

_____

_____

_____

_____

Excuses are often fears disguised as reasons. How can you get those fears away from your dreams this week?

_____

_____

_____

_____

_____

_____

_____

_____

_____

Do not let your hearts be troubled, neither let them
be afraid. [Stop allowing yourselves to be agitated
and disturbed; and do not permit yourselves to be
fearful and intimidated and cowardly and unsettled.]
—JOHN 14:27, AMP

This week, as you focus on making progress on your dreams, note successes and challenges below.

48

In the world you have tribulation and trials and distress and frustration; but be of good cheer [take courage; be confident, certain, undaunted]! For I have overcome the world. [I have deprived it of power to harm you and have conquered it for you.]
—JOHN 16:33, AMP

What I am working on this week for dream number one (taken from your most recent action steps):

_____

_____

_____

_____

_____

_____

What I am working on this week for dream number two:

_____

_____

_____

_____

_____

What I am working on this week for dream number three:

_____

_____

_____

_____

_____

This week, focus on making specific progress on your dreams. Note successes and challenges below.

49

> You crown the year with Your goodness,
> and Your paths drip with abundance.
> —PSALM 65:11

This week, start to integrate your dream design into whatever tools you use to manage your time: a calendar, your computer schedule, notes, reminders, etc. Each of your remaining steps probably contain several action items, so keep breaking your dream design apart into smaller daily and weekly pieces.

Specific ways I can do this:

This week, take time to pause and consider your progress. Write your impressions below:

50

...for it is God Who is all the while effectually at work in you [energizing and creating in you the power and desire], both to will and to work for His good pleasure and satisfaction and delight.
—Philippians 2:13, amp

What I am working on this week for dream number one (taken from your most recent action steps):

_____

_____

_____

_____

_____

_____

What I am working on this week for dream number two:

_____

_____

_____

_____

_____

_____

What I am working on this week for dream number three:

_____

_____

_____

_____

_____

_____

This week, focus on making specific progress on your dreams. Note successes and challenges below.

51

You're already seeing your dreams becoming real!

This week, continue to transfer your dream design into whatever tools you use to help manage your time. Include positive reminders and scriptures.

Each of your remaining steps can contain several action items, so keep breaking your dream design apart into smaller daily and weekly pieces.

Specific ways I can do this:

_____

_____

_____

_____

_____

_____

_____

_____

_____

_____

_____

_____

_____

_____

_____

_____

_____

_____

_____

_____

_____

_____

This week, take time to pause and consider your progress. Write your impressions below:

52

With God all things are possible.
—MARK 10:27

What I am working on this week for dream number one (taken from your most recent action steps):

_____

_____

_____

_____

_____

_____

What I am working on this week for dream number two:

_____

_____

_____

_____

_____

What I am working on this week for dream number three:

_____

_____

_____

_____

_____

_____

At whatever stage you find yourself, pause and note how your faith, persistence, and God's faithfulness have contributed to the success of your dream journey.

_____

_____

_____

_____

_____

_____

_____

_____

_____

_____

_____

_____

_____

_____

_____

_____

_____

_____

_____

_____

_____

This week, transfer all your dream designs into whatever tools you use to manage your time. Include positive reminders and scriptures.

Each of your remaining steps can contain several action items, so keep breaking your dream design apart into smaller daily and weekly pieces.

Congratulations, dreamer!

You've reached the end of this journal.

By now you know that the adventure never ends! As each dream is accomplished, God will give you even bigger dreams. As you reflect on your journey so far, continue moving forward until you've accomplished everything He has placed in your heart.

And remember to focus on what you can do, and don't get bogged down with what you can't do right now.

Most importantly, I hope you've discovered the dream person you were designed to be—created in God's image to dream and live big!

Keep dreaming!

Art Sepúlveda

Notes

1. Orisen Swett Marden, *Peace, Power and Plenty* (n.p.: Kensington Publishing LLC, 2003), 202.
2. Cybernation.com, "Thomas Carlyle," http://www.cybernation.com/victory/quotations/authors/quotes_carlyle_thomas.html (accessed May 7, 2008).
3. John Maxwell, *Thinking for a Change* (New York: Warner Business Books, 2003), 69.
4. Van Crouch, *Winning 101* (Tulsa, OK: Honor Books, 1988), 56–57.
5. Ken Blanchard and Spencer Johnson, *The One Minute Manager* (New York: The Berkley Publishing Group, 1981).

Journal

_____

_____

_____

_____

_____

_____

_____

_____

_____

_____

_____

_____

_____

_____

_____

_____

_____

_____

_____

_____

_____

_____

_____

_____

_____

_____

_____

Journal

Journal

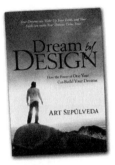

For more information
about the author or
Word of Life Christian Center
please visit us online at

www.wordoflifehawaii.com

Or write us at
550 Queen Street
Honolulu, HI 96813

wolcc@wolhawaii.com